RENISHAW HALL

has been the home of the SITWELL family for nearly 400 years and in recent decades has become famous through the writings of Edith, Osbert and Sacheverell, the three gifted children of the eccentric Sir George and Lady Ida Sitwell. The youngest of the 'trio', 'Sachie' (1897-1988), was the only one of his generation to marry and Renishaw now belongs to his elder son, Sir Reresby Sitwell, seventh baronet of Renishaw: it is still a family home.

Sir Reresby and Lady Sitwell

'Cecil Beaton's romantic photos of Edith, [...] in establishing their images as a trio of ecc[...] straightforwardly, he photographs the who[...] is second from left; next to him, on a Vene[...] Sitwell sits on her knee. "Sachie" stands b[...] the right; Georgia, wife of Sachie and mot[...]'

Photograph courtesy of Sotheby's, London.

1

For
Aziza
with love from us both
Reresby. 12.10.01

A BRIEF HISTORY OF
RENISHAW AND THE SITWELLS

Renishaw cannot claim to be an architectural gem, nor on first sight is it improved by the grim industrial surroundings: many people will be daunted by the weather-beaten and gloomy north façade of the ancient building. Moreover, it is no surprise to learn that the house has the sinister reputation of being haunted, an aspect that has not been blurred by the peculiar circumstances of history, as will emerge from these notes; for Renishaw has not been lived in throughout every room nor all the year round for well over a century. Again, Renishaw had only two owners between 1862, the year that Sir George succeeded in his infancy and 1965, when the late Sir Osbert 'abdicated' in favour of his elder nephew, Reresby, so that makes only three owners between 1862 and year 2001, (so far). Perhaps these are factors that may contribute to the strange compelling atmosphere which seems always to have held a mysterious grip upon all who live or work here, an enchantment that will not appeal to everyone - and may well be tempered by the vagaries of climate - but has led one visitor, the artist, Rex Whistler, to declare that Renishaw *was the most exciting place he knew.*

And the red reynard creeps
to his hole near the river
the copper leaves fall
and the bare trees shiver

From 'Winter The Huntsman' by Osbert Sitwell

3

Renishaw from the Lime Avenue

Set in garden and parkland, Renishaw is barely two miles from the M1 motorway and equidistant about 155 miles - between London and the nearest point on the Scottish border. Eastward lies Sherwood Forest with its thousand lingering memories of Robin Hood and the 'Dukeries'; to the west the land rises steeply towards the Peak National Park, southwards are the hills and dales of Derbyshire, mixed farming and coal mining; while, only six miles to the north is the heart of the great sprawling city of Sheffield - for Renishaw is on the fringes of Hallamshire, 'that southern corner of the West Riding where Yorkshire ends, where Derbyshire begins and of which Sheffield is the natural centre and capital'. Older people may remember Renishaw as a green oasis in the industrial deserts but in recent years the coal mines have all closed and the iron works have gone; the countryside is greener yet Renishaw remains.

Even before the Romans, this was a border region: to the north lay the country of the Brigantes, to the south the land of the Coritani. After the departure of the Roman legions, one tribal host of Saxon invaders spread northwards from Derby and settled this shire to form part of the Kingdom of Mercia that stretched thus far. A few miles away is Dore, the 'door' into Northumbria, where Egbert, victorious King of the West Saxons, came against Eanfrith, the Northern King, in the year 829. The Northumbrians proceeded with caution rather than valour and decided to accept Egbert as overlord, so the two armies disbanded in peace and from this momentous confrontation dates the union of England as one country.

Sitwells appear early at Ridgeway, three miles from Renishaw and, until Victorian times, also part of the extensive parish of Eckington. In 1301 an old lawsuit finds here Simon Sitwell, first of the name, and declares him to be the rightful son and heir of a certain Walter de Boys, or de Bosco ('of the Wood'), who had died on pilgrimage to the Holy Land. In 1310 Roger Cytewelle was one of the founders of the Guild of St. Mary of Eckington, and by the middle of that century the Sitwells were installed in the main village.

Robert Sytwell is probably the youngish man dressed in the fashion of Edward VI in the earliest family portrait. He had moved around 1540 to Staveley Netherthorpe, three miles away to the south. Later on he acquired the site of the present house at Renishaw by buying up certain closes originally part of the great common ryecroft in the 'South Field' of Eckington, perhaps with the intention he never carried out of building there; for he continued to live at Staveley, where he helped to found the local grammar school in 1572. Considered a rich man in his day, he had lease of a coal mine at Eckington Marsh as early as 1560 and was one of 48 residents of Derbyshire who contributed to the defence of the realm against the Spanish Armada - two forked up as much as £50 and he was among four that produced £25. Perhaps patriotism was tempered by religious beliefs, for his name had also appeared in a list of *principall recusants in com. Derby, 1587.* 'Ould' Robert died childless in 1599 and made things awkward for his cousin and heir by leaving all that he could of his numerous properties to his young Catholic widow, tenants and servants, *recusants* all. Years of litigation ensued: the elderly Protestant cousin 'being an old man and weary of the strife' made over his claims to his son, who managed to consolidate the Eckington estates but died only two years after his weary father, leaving an infant son.

George Sitwell, first to be described as 'of Renishaw' was born in 1600, a year after his grandfather had succeeded to the disputed fortunes of Robert Sytwell of Staveley. From the savings effected during his long minority he built himself an H-shaped manor house of the *Pennine* type, gabled and battlemented, that forms the central nucleus of the present house, and moved in with his bride, Margaret Childers, in 1625. During the Civil Wars he garrisoned Renishaw for the King and so was continually fined as a *persistent delinquent* under Cromwell's regime but was able to recover, thanks to handsome profits from the iron works that he had started, an enterprise that largely enhanced the family fortunes. Indeed, by the end of the century the Sitwells were the greatest makers of iron nails in the world and *one tenth* of the entire output of the iron trade in England passed through their hands.

The Squires of Renishaw in the seventeenth and eighteenth centuries were Whigs, quiet and scholarly country gentlemen who collected books and pictures, improved the farming and planting of the estate, amassed rents and royalties and married heiresses - hence the strange family names affected by later generations.

Younger sons were put into trade and many worked so hard they never found time to marry, so left their fortunes back to their eldest brother or nephew: the younger sons of the old cavalier and ironmaster were Robert, a cloth merchant in Aleppo and George, a silk merchant in Spain while John, the youngest and scape-grace of the family - and, of course, his father's favourite - was at one time apprenticed to a tailor in Derby.

Francis Sitwell, second owner of Renishaw, married Katherine Sacheverell of an old Norman family, once well known in Derbyshire and Nottinghamshire but long extinct. They produced a large family but he died young in 1671, having survived his father only four years. Next to the monument to his parents in Eckington church is a plain wall tablet with this touching epitaph:-

*Here death hath laid my treasure up
This earth doth cover
my cordial friend my loyal
Spouse and faithfull lover.*

My Rent Book Begining whitsuntide 1678 is witness to the business-like methods of his widow, who was sister to William Sacheverell, creator of the Whig party and described by Speaker Onslow as 'the ablest parliament man' of his time; he was guardian to his nephew George, who succeeded to Renishaw at the age of ten.

'Mr. Justice' Sitwell's portraits show a high-bridged nose and formidable periwig; his letters confirm the stern principles and strong temper inherited from his uncle. He took a minor part in the 'English Revolution' of 1688 when the Whigs forced James II to abdicate and replaced him with his son-in-law and nephew, William of Orange, George Sitwell being made a *Commissioner* for the City of London at the time of the *coup d'état*. He and his wife Anne, daughter and heiress of Thomas Kent of Povey, have left no living descendants for only one of their several children married; Alice, who was to wed her first cousin and

5

become mother of two sickly boys who died young and of whom one has become famous as

'The Boy in Pink', Henry, last of the Sacheverells, said to be the little ghost that wakens ladies with his cold kisses from beyond the grave. He was the last of the Sacheverells and died in 1726 aged 13.

Francis, next owner of Renishaw, was a bachelor who had 'declared against matrimony' as, it seems, did both his younger brothers and two first cousins along with his sister Elizabeth, who left her fortune to a Wilmot cousin, ancestor of the numerous Wilmot-Sitwells. George - yet another younger son to be named after his father and be put into trade - purchased property at Whiston near Rotherham, still part of the estate. Thomas, the youngest, became a clergyman and Fellow of Corpus Christi College, Cambridge, and engaged in lengthy and sometimes pedantic correspondence with his brothers. Scholarly and house-proud, Francis Sitwell carried out various alterations to both house and garden, most of which have been swept away; his main surviving legacy consists of his library of books on astronomy, mathematics and the classics; he died in 1753 and was succeeded by yet another bachelor, his elderly cousin William, who had grown rich in commerce in London.

William Sitwell was the younger son of a younger son, an earlier William, brother of 'Mr. Justice' Sitwell, who had married Mary Reresby, eventual heiress of that ancient family, and settled in Sheffield, where they produced two

sons, also bachelors; another Francis, who was a highly successful lawyer but died young, and William, the merchant. In about 1960 two old tin boxes of legal documents turned up mysteriously from the vaults of the Goldsmiths' Hall in London: one set of papers dealt with an action that William Sitwell won over a ship that he had insured but which sank in harbour before it had ever set sail. He loved music and the theatre, and lived little at Renishaw, preferring Bath and London, where he indulged in his favourite philanthropical and charitable works. When he died, William Sitwell was said to have been one of the richest men in the City, worth £500,000, and with him the direct male line came to an end.

Francis Hurt, only son of Johnathan Hurt and Catherine Sitwell, succeeded to his uncle William's fortune and estates and changed his name to Sitwell in 1777. Jonathan Hurt, it is known, was the only surviving son of Valentine Hurt of Hesley Hall, near Sheffield, by Mary, daughter and heiress of John Saxton; his grandfather was Nicholas Hurt, who had been one of the agents of the great Thomas Wentworth, Earl of Strafford and had died and been buried in the chapel at Wentworth in

1653, Jonathan's grandmother being the second of Nicholas Hurt's three wives, Margaret, daughter and co-heiress of Matthew Stafford of Wortley. Beyond Nicholas all is uncertain and mere conjecture: legal proofs of his own parentage are missing but it is *assumed* that he descended from the Hurts of Haldworth who *may* have been a younger branch of the Hurts of Ashbourne and Alderwasley (pronounced *"Aller's Lea"*). If the earlier Sitwells, however worthy and relatively long-established were, frankly, rather obscure, there is little evidence from which to judge the Hurts, so dim and fragmentary are their records. Yet, compared with their sober and industrious predecessors, the Hurts seem to have had a wild streak in their blood, for the scholarly squires and merchants of Stuart and early Georgian times were to be followed by great sportsmen, and Whigs by Tories with Jacobite sympathies - the portraits of William and Mary of Orange were banished upstairs to the attic landing where they remain.

Francis Hurt Sitwell, as he came to be known, had been born and brought up in Sheffield, then a picturesque old market town, by his widowed mother and grandmother, 'Madam' Sitwell, *née* Reresby, who

Francis Hurt, only son of Jonathan Hurt and Catherine Sitwell, succeeded to his uncle William's fortune and estates and changed his name to Sitwell in 1777.

both died within two years of his uncle inheriting Renishaw, whereupon William Sitwell adopted him, and uncle and nephew moved around between Renishaw, London, Bath and other watering places. He shared his uncle's taste for music and played both flute and violin: many of his music-books are preserved at Renishaw, winter evenings were enlivened by music parties. In 1766 the younger man began paying his addresses to Mary, daughter of Canon Warneford of York, described as the 'Beauty of Bath' and a very clever, intellectual girl besides - what at that time was

called a *précieuse* - they married and so the musical bandwagon increased. A few years after his uncle's death, Francis Hurt Sitwell also inherited from his cousin, Samuel Phipps, large landed estates in Northumberland, Shropshire and South Yorkshire that were eventually parcelled out among his three sons, the boys in the portrait group he commissioned from John Singleton Copley. In 1792 he sold the iron works and died the following year. He was succeeded at Renishaw by his eldest son, twice a Sitwell by name, whose passion for outdoor sports and mania for building immediately became apparent. For the three next generations lived hard and died young; vast sums were spent in enlarging the house and entertaining; ultimately they lost the bulk of their inheritance.

Sitwell Sitwell was a man of exceptional energy in several directions. He married twice: hardly was he of age when he became engaged to Alice Parke, daughter of a Liverpool merchant. His parents opposed the match at first, although the girl's mother came of an old Lancashire family, the Prestons of Preston, and her brother was to eclipse them all, for he rose to great

7

eminence in the law, as the famous judge, Lord Wensleydale who through his three pretty daughters became grandfather of the 9th Earl of Carlisle and of the first Viscounts Ridley and Ullswater. Two portraits, one by Sir William Beechey, exist at Renishaw of the delicate, fair-haired Alice Sitwell, who produced a son and heir, and died two weeks later. In the following year, 1798, her widower married Caroline Stovin, later celebrated as the 'Blue-Stocking' Lady Sitwell, friend of every literary man from Byron to Longfellow; she left him no children but he had others by various mistresses. We must now turn to Mr. Sitwell's building activities.

In 1793 the dining room was added and two years later the classical stables were built to accommodate both the horses and a pack of harriers which once gave chase to two 'Royal Bengal' tigers that had escaped from a menagerie in Sheffield. Sitwell Sitwell also owned a choice collection of fighting cocks. In 1803 the other end of the house was embellished with a great new drawing-room, a billiard room and finally, in 1808, the ballroom beyond, completed with the Prince of Wales's feathers on the ceiling to commemorate a ball given in

honour of the Prince Regent, who afterwards made his host a baronet. Sir Sitwell Sitwell employed Joseph Badger of Sheffield, a comparatively unknown local architect but this was the time when English taste was at its best. The Gothick Temple and ruined Lodge on the drive are believed, however, to have been built to Sir Sitwell's own designs, shortly afterwards he died suddenly at the early age of 41 in 1811, and was succeeded by his only son, the first Sir George.

Sir George's trustees sold the racing stud 'on the premises' - in fact, in the so-called *Top Paddock*, where the vineyard is now situated - but the hunters and hounds were kept on and soon Sir George was living at the same rate as his father. He married Susan Tait, eldest sister to Archibald Campbell Tait, first Scotsman to become Archbishop of Canterbury; their paternal grandmother had been a Miss Murdoch, who bore the unusual Christian name, for a female, of *Charles*, for she came of a family that had lost everything in the Jacobite cause yet still in their reverses remained loyal to the Young Pretender, so she had been named after him. The new Lady Sitwell, who, as a bride had been described

'with her showers of golden or light auburn hair, her peculiarly slight and graceful figure, her large happy blue eyes and lips like a rose', bore altogether nine children. She encouraged her husband to be one of the first Englishmen to go to Scotland for the shooting; for several years they took a lease first of Birkhall and then of Balmoral - before, of course, Queen Victoria 'discovered' the Highlands. Meanwhile, from 1818 onwards for thirty years, the Taits, a numerous sept, made Renishaw headquarters for their various campaigns; relying on Sir George's weak, kindly and sociable disposition, hordes of indigent Scottish relations poured down and the burden of this expense thrust upon Sir George contributed to his ruin.

Financial disasters followed. Farm rents had fallen since the Napoleonic Wars, a solicitor robbed Sir George of a fortune, he lost money over a contract and fought an expensive election in which a local newspaper in the Radical interest addressed him as *Thou art the King of Tories, 0 Geordie, the fox-hunting son of a cock-fighting father*. Finally, in 1848 the Sheffield Bank failed. Much of the estate and contents of the house were sold but the pictures, tapestries and beds, and the original oak furniture in the hall were reserved. Sir George found himself obliged to live on £700 a year instead of the £12,000 to which he had been accustomed. The family left Renishaw and travelled abroad for two years, visiting small German courts, such as Wiesbaden, and going on to Nice, then still Piedmontese territory. They returned to England to live at Bognor and Sir George never revisited Renishaw, except for two nights in the winter before he died in 1853.

Sir Reresby Sitwell, 3rd Baronet, succeeded, aged 33, and suffered an even shorter and unhappier life than his immediate predecessors. He inherited what remained of the Renishaw estates, burdened with the large charges appropriate to a great fortune, and with first call on the income. His six surviving brothers and sisters had to be provided for in accordance with arrangements made many years before, while his step-grandmother, the Blue-Stocking, though her first husband had died in 1811 and she was now married, again to a rich man, was drawing a steady jointure of £3,000 a year and continued to do so in all for 50 years. Further, Sir Reresby had been induced to make

himself responsible for his father's very considerable debts. The result of this was that the former handsome and carefree young cornet in The First Life Guards, worn down by fatigue, overwhelmed by worry for the future of his wife and infants, and unable to see his way out of the tangle in which he was caught, fell an easy victim to illness and died, like his grandfather, at the early age of 41.

His young widow was one of the five daughters of Col. the Hon. Henry Hely-Hutchinson, a veteran of Waterloo and brother of the third Earl of Donoughmore. She was an Irish Protestant, a lady of intense religious inclinations but sound business sense. She found herself with two very young children - another daughter had died in extreme infancy - in a large, old-fashioned house, shorn of many of its treasures, and which she could not afford to keep up properly. And so, in this moment, fraught as it seemed with the loss of all worldly happiness, she retired to Scarborough, there to bring up her children and to devote herself to religious and philanthropic work; while at the same time, in the years between his

father's death and attaining his majority, by her clever management she contrived to pull the family estates round for her son, the second Sir George, that rather unusual personage who was grandfather of the present owner.

The discovery of coal in large quantities deep below the southern fringes of the park served to restore the family fortunes at least as efficaciously as the stringent economies and prudent stewardship of the widowed Louisa Lucy, Lady Sitwell. As we have noted, Sitwells had exploited first coal and then iron long before the Industrial Revolution, in which they failed to participate. The construction of the Chesterfield canal some 100 years previously heralded the advance of progress, followed by the coming of the railways. The family newspaper had recorded the memorable appearance of the 'first small train-full', the youthful reporter conjectured, 'of directors and engineers - steaming through the green meadow beside the little river. It was to us all a marvellous sight, and soon the lawn was dotted with the gardeners, stablemen, workmen and others, who came flying in the wildest excitement to witness it, but', she lamented, 'the railway cut

9

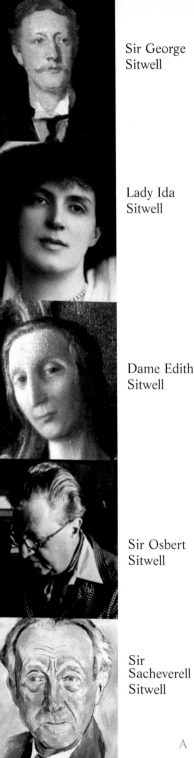

Sir George
Sitwell

Lady Ida
Sitwell

Dame Edith
Sitwell

Sir Osbert
Sitwell

Sir
Sacheverell
Sitwell

off almost a third of the park, and interfered with sport.'

Oh what would our fox-hunting forefathers say,
If they saw through the coverts and grounds,
Steam carriages whizzing by night and by day,
But no huntsmen, no horses, no hounds!

Renishaw began to assume its aspect of a 'green oasis among the industrial deserts', yet its inmates, if seemingly isolated with their religious and later intellectual preoccupations, were acutely aware of the grim realities of life among the industrial proletariat around them. Charity for their poorer neighbours seems also to have been coupled with envy of the Seely, Stephenson and other richer but more recently established families who had sullied their hands in trade and cashed in on industrial developments.

Meanwhile, the great house on top of the hill slumbered under dust-sheets for many cold months every year; much fine furniture, nearly all the silver and most of the books in the library had gone in the great sales of 1847, along with many broad acres of farmland. Not surprisingly, the fairy-tale gothick building with weather-beaten fabric and vast, half-empty rooms, gradually acquired the reputation of being haunted and yet while so many hundreds of other English country houses were ruined in the heyday of Victorian affluence and bad taste, Renishaw eventually emerged to preserve

intact much of its Stuart and Regency past.

Sir George Reresby Sitwell, fourth baronet, has acquired a certain celebrity, thanks to the writings of his three children. Born in 1860, he succeeded at the age of two, so could not remember his own father, and was brought up in a stifling atmosphere of family prayers, good works and enforced economies at home. He reacted to become a convinced atheist and combine both parsimony and personal extravagance in equal if unpredictable measures. He ruled the roost for eighty-one years, that is longer than the reigns of all four previous generations and despite his life-long hypochondria, had to admit that he had been Lord of the Manor of Eckington for more years than any single one of his predecessors, all of whom   he had made it his business to identify and date since the reign of Ethelred the Unready. His austere habits conflicted   with the more frivolous instincts of his beautiful young wife, Lady Ida Emily Augusta Denison, whom he married in 1886. Her father was Earl of Londesborough and her mother daughter of the 7th Duke of Beaufort by his first Duchess, a niece of Wellington, and she was also descended from Lady Conyngham, the favourite of George IV. The offspring of this ill-matched but lasting union were the three writers who have added lustre to the family name: Dame Edith (1887-1964), Sir Osbert (1892-1969) and Sir Sacheverell Sitwell (1897-1988).

Sir George inherited both the scholarly tastes of his remoter ancestors and the latter-day mania for building. He spent most of his life in study of medieval history, genealogy and heraldry, architecture and gardening, only occasionally emerging from his ivory tower to have yet another book of indigestible content printed on his private press, or to pick fault with his family and dependants and play the tyrant. An unsympathetic husband and a trying and difficult parent, he is also revered as a benevolent and understanding grandfather.

Sir George's main achievements, indeed the only of many schemes and enterprises to be completed and reach fruition, were his essay *On the Making of Gardens*, an acknowledged little masterpiece, and the formal gardens and lakes at Renishaw. As soon as he came of age he began to plan a whole series of improvements, together with further additions to the house and new buildings (few of which, mercifully, ever left the drawing board), under the restraint rather than the guidance of his friend, Sir Edwin Lutyens. The stories of his many eccentricities and quixotic whims are recounted in the works of his children, more especially in the five monumental volumes of his elder son Sir Osbert's autobiography, *Left Hand, Right Hand!*

In 1909 Sir George bought the vast Castle of Montegufoni in the hills of Tuscany, off the old road from Florence to Volterra. He and his crony, the Signor 'Bracciaforte' of Sir Osbert's memoirs, spent the next thirty years restoring and refurnishing the Castle *as it might have been* in the days of its former owners, the Acciaiuoli, Florentine bankers and Dukes of Athens in the Middle Ages. Eventually Sir George and Lady Ida were persuaded to go and live permanently at Montegufoni by their children and 'make over' the two family houses and properties in England.

Osbert, the elder son took on Renishaw and "Sachie" the younger son, got Weston the smaller house in Northamptonshire, inherited from an aunt of Sir George. Sachie married Georgia Doble, daughter of a Montreal banker.

'Captain Osbert', as he was affectionately known in north-east Derbyshire between the wars, having survived the rigours of an unhappy childhood being *educated during the holidays from Eton*' and all the horrors of trench warfare, settled into Renishaw during the twenties. For the next forty-four years it remained his summer headquarters from which he 'conducted, in conjunction with his brother and sister, a series of skirmishes and hand-to-hand battles against the Philistine'. Despite their removal to Italy, Sir George and Lady Ida came over most years to visit their sons and the whole family would forgather at Renishaw, complete with hangers-on, governesses and servants for a few weeks under the kindly if cynical eye of their host.

Lady Ida died in 1937, Sir George retired to Montegufoni and the Second War came. Lack of his favourite food, roast chicken, as much as the occupying troops forced him to retreat to Switzerland, where he died in 1943. During the war years Sir Osbert concentrated on his autobiography, which was illustrated by the famous series of paintings by John Piper that adorn his study and other rooms at

Renishaw. After the war he basked for a while in public acclaim (Sir Arthur Bryant hailed him *as the greatest living master of English prose*) and he and Dame Edith made triumphant lecture tours of the United States. However, the symptoms of that mysterious and harrowing complaint known as Parkinson's Disease became evident and for the last twenty years of his life Sir Osbert became increasingly infirm and dependent on his nurses. Even so his physical courage, high spirits and humour never failed him to the very end. In 1965, like his father before him, Sir Osbert was prevailed upon to give up Renishaw; he made the house and family estates over to his elder nephew, and retired to Montegufoni, where he died in 1969.

Sir Reresby Sitwell, Bt., D.L., was born 15th April, 1927, and brought up by his parents at the other family home, Weston Hall in Northamptonshire. Black Nannah was succeeded by a French-Swiss governess, then came the rigours of a 'private' school, followed by wartime Eton, where he won a scholarship in mediaeval history to King's College, Cambridge. After three years in the Grenadier Guards, mainly spent serving as a Lieutenant in the British Army of the Rhine, he went up to Cambridge but left of his own volition without a degree. From 1948 to 1963 Reresby worked in advertising and public relations, and for several years operated a vending machine business. Since 1964 he has also been active in the wine trade and planted the vineyard at Renishaw in 1972. He has not followed in the family footsteps, apart from this booklet, and collaborating with John Julius Norwich and A. Costa in 1964 to produce *Mount Athos*, an illustrated record of that strange land of monks where no woman, child or eunuch is admitted and, more recently, contributing an epilogue to *Hortus Sitwellianus*, a family compendium on gardening. Reresby served as High Sheriff of Derbyshire for the year 1983-4, the 677th to hold that ancient office since records began with Osbert Sylvanus in 1129; in 1984 he was given the Freedom of the City of London and appointed a Deputy Lieutenant for Derbyshire. In 1988 Sir Sacheverell died aged 90, and his elder son Reresby succeeded as 7th Baronet. He is a member of White's, Brooks's and Pratt's Clubs and is a member of the Society of Dilettanti.

Lady Sitwell, A.L.C.M., is the younger daughter of the late Colonel the Honble. Donald Forbes, D.S.O., M.V.O. and Mrs. Forbes. She is a niece of the eighth Earl of Granard and her mother, who was a Miss Lawson of Aldborough in Yorkshire, is a granddaughter of the fourteenth Viscount Mountgarret so, like the two previous *châtelaines* of Renishaw, Penelope is thus part-Irish and part-Yorkshire. Sadly, she has given up the piano but is a keen needlewoman and nowadays she is passionately addicted to gardening; she also runs a single-handed antique business, *Southwick Antiques*, trading mainly in Chinese vases and lamps. Alexandra, only child of Penelope and Reresby, is married to Richard, elder son of multi-millionaire entrepreneur and philanthropist Sir 'Union' Jack Hayward. Alexandra and Rick have two children Rosaleen ('Rosie') born 1993 and Osbert ('Bertie') born 1994. The Sitwells spend much time in London, where Penelope owns a house near Hyde Park and, like so many earlier Sitwells, they share a love of travel and sightseeing but are seldom happier than when they return to Renishaw, which for the first time for over a century is now opened up at all times of year and here they come to supervise repairs and redecorating, install a few innovations, and entertain their friends.

RENISHAW ROOM BY ROOM

The ancient building straddles the crest of a hill: the approach drives wind up through parkland past gaunt old trees that stand sentinel around the entrance front. Grey and machicolated, this grim northern façade is of immense length and decidedly 'Gothick' character, concealing the narrow width of the house and the beautiful garden beyond of terraced lawns, clipped yew hedges and pyramids, statues and fountains, that lies on the southern aspect.

Above:
Rex Whistler's design for
Renishaw Hall's letterheading.

the FRONT HALL

We go in by the front door - the only entrance on this side - into the Front Hall, the central focus of the house, that occupies most of the ground floor of the original building of 1625 and begin our tour. Two late 17th century carved and painted wooden figures of warriors confront the visitor, one scowling and the other grinning, they are a foretaste of many objects Venetian in origin or inspiration. Beyond the warriors the eye travels to the large open fire blazing at the far end of the hall; ranged around are a series of oak chairs, settees, dressers and gate-leg tables, all made for the house in the middle of the 17th century and a

Osbert Sitwell by Frank Dobson, 1921-1922. Osbert Sitwell sat for Frank Dobson nearly every day for three months.

cradle inscribed 'Henry and Ianet Sitwell, 25 days IVNE, 1667'. Over the fireplace is a large canvas in oils, depicting various Venetian scenes, by John Piper, the side walls display another composite scene *Derbyshire Domains*, this time of Renishaw and other great houses in the neighbourhood, a 'roofscape' of the house, also smaller views of Renishaw and of Bolsover Castle, all by the same artist. On our tour we will have to cross in and out of the Front Hall: so, retracing our steps back towards the warriors by the entrance, we notice a series of archways, two on either side, flanked by 17th and 18th century portraits. Under one archway that leads to the foot of the Main Stairs are hung some of the earliest family

documents and one of special interest, perhaps: a *Protection* granted by Ferdinando, Lord Fairfax, 'Lord General of the North' to George Sitwell, builder of this central nucleus of the house, when he surrendered the place to the Roundheads on 9th August, 1644. The Renishaw archives are remarkably complete and the selection on display is continued under the opposite pair of archways and beyond in the Smoke Room, our next port of call.

Opposite: In 1969 a visitor left his spectacles in the Hall and Sir Reresby put them on the figure, hoping that if the visitor returned he would retrieve his glasses. They are still here to this day.

14

the SMOKE ROOM

The Smoke Room is first mentioned in 1730 - the name records the etiquette of long ago - it is a lobby that connects the Front Hall with two service passages. Newly painted red with a modern Turkish carpet of mediaeval Seljuk pattern to match, the main feature is a recent double portrait of the present owners by Paul Benney, surrounded by more portraits of ancestors, more oak furniture with a fine mid-18th century Chinese cabinet. Over the door facing the windows is a treasured possession of questioned authenticity - none other than Robin Hood's bow: by it is framed an old letter giving its reputed history; beneath further 17th and 18th century portraits are hung other documents of varying interest and amusement, some of recent date.

The newly painted Smoke Room incorporating the recent double portrait of the present owners by Paul Benney.

the ANTE-DINING ROOM

The Ante-Dining Room is much the smallest of the ground-floor 'reception' rooms with only two windows that look out on to the garden. Around the oval gate-leg table is a set of six Venetian chairs of around 1700, made not in the city itself but in some provincial workshop on the mainland. The two finest Dutch paintings in the house are here: a portrait of a lady with a little girl, both wearing lace of the finest application, signed and dated 'Cornelius Johnson, 1621' and a street scene featuring the Stadhuis at s'Hertogenbosch (Bois-le-Duc) by Jan Abrahamsz Beerstraaten signed and dated 1665. In a gothic frame is a painting of *Saint Sebastian* by Orcagna (1308-1368). *The Madonna and Child* (below right) is a painting by Sebastiano di Bartolo Mainardi, who was born in San Gimignano *c*. 1450. He became the favourite pupil and brother-in-law of Domenico Ghirlandaio and died in Florence in 1515. In a niche between the windows stands a circular cabinet 'custom-built' to contain the glass goblet engraved by Laurence Whistler with a view of the sombre and symmetrical north façade of Renishaw and inscription that this was commissioned by the Society of Authors 'For Sir Osbert Sitwell in gratitude for all he has done for his fellow writers', dated 1946.

Above the fireplace is a fine Dutch portrait by Cornelius Johnson, 1621, of a lady with a little girl both wearing lace of the finest application.

17

the DINING ROOM

The Dining Room is the first of the great additions to the house made by Sitwell Sitwell, later first baronet, and was completed in 1793. Built in four bays, the room culminates in an apse or domed recess that was contrived to incorporate the former cockpit and was designed by a little-known architect, Joseph Badger of Sheffield, who later built on to the other end of the house the Great Drawing Room (1803), the so-called Billiard Room and the Ballroom (1808), besides various other buildings in and around the park, notably the fine classical Stables (1795).

*'The Dining Room -
a rare interior'* by
John Piper.

The immense cabinet facing the apse, on the left as one enters, is of mid-17th century Neapolitan workmanship with glass panels painted with classical scenes.

The decoration of this room is the most elaborate at Renishaw: ionic pilasters flank the apse and its ceiling is plastered in a classical motif of roses and wreaths or chaplets of smaller flowers. The ceiling of the main part of the room has a feathered pattern in the centre from which radiate further designs of feathers and concentric rings of chaplets, repeated at the four corners: beneath is a cornice decorated with honeysuckle that reappear along the dado and over the four fine mahogany doors. Two large conversation pieces dominate the room among various other family portraits, a typical Dutch church interior, *The Ballad Seller* by Henry Walton, and two beautiful rococo looking-glasses between the end and central pairs of windows. Over the chimneypiece hangs *A Young Lady and her Brothers* by John Singleton Copley (1787) and, on the adjacent wall opposite the apse, an early nineteenth century family group by John Partridge. The three brothers in the Copley painting are the progenitors of the three main branches of the family. On the right is the eldest boy, Sitwell Sitwell himself: running across the centre is the youngest, Hurt, who was to inherit Ferney Hall in Shropshire, long since burned down and this line almost extinct; on the left lolls the ne'er-do-well Frank, aged only eight in the painting, already holding a deck of cards; he grew to found the Barmoor Sitwells, most numerous today, and to gamble away many wide acres of Northumberland. The next owner of Renishaw is shown in the group by Partridge: Sir George Sitwell, second baronet, is the proud young father in hunting clothes, seen with his wife and growing family in about 1828. The individual portraits include works by Sir Godfrey Kneller and members of the Verelst family, notably *The Boy in Pink* Henry, last of the Sacheverells, the most famous ghost that haunts this place.

the LIBRARY

The Library, once the 'Great Parlour', like its counterpart the Ante-Dining Room, formerly 'Little Parlour', was part of the original 17th century manor house of modest proportions and the ceiling still retains its quaint Jacobean plastering of geometrical patterns, dotted with squirrels, mermaids, lions' heads, vine leaves and so on. The two wall niches that contain large majolica vases were once windows looking out to the east. The conversation piece over the fireplace is *The Cherry Barrow*, painted by Henry Walton and purchased by his friend Francis Hurt Sitwell at the opening of the Royal Academy in 1768.

22

the GREAT DRAWINGROOM

The Great Drawingroom was built by Joseph Badger for Sitwell Sitwell in 1803 and is nearly 70 feet long with seven huge windows, two looking south and five to the east. The proportions are, perhaps, even finer than those of the Dining Room built ten years earlier but the decoration is much more restrained. We are told that the central ornament of the ceiling was finished by a plasterer named Holiday and that here the youthful Francis Chantrey from the neighbouring village of Norton 'not only saw the practice and talked about the art of modelling but first tried his prentice hand on plastic materials'. The resulting scheme is an unambitious version of the feather design with rays and concentric chaplets that draws the eye to the heavy Regency gilt-bronze colza-oil chandelier, fitted since 1968 with electric bulbs. Main feature of this room is, of course, the magnificent commode, attributed to the designs of Robert Adam and the workmanship of Thomas Chippendale with vignettes by the Swedish craftsman Fuhlvohg and ormolu mounts by Matthew Bolton. Over the commode hangs an attractive silhouette of the Sitwell and Warneford families by Torond, *c.* 1776, and above this the celebrated conversation piece of 1900-01 by John Singer Sargent (1856-1925) of Sir George Sitwell, fourth baronet, his wife Lady Ida and their three famous children Edith, Osbert and Sacheverell - respectively grandparents, aunt, uncle and father of the present owner of Renishaw. On either side of the Sargent group - painted, of course, as a companion piece to the other great painting in the house by an American, the Copley - hang two vast tapestries from the series of five by a Brussels tapissier, Judocus de Vos, who worked on allegorical scenes from cartoons by Le Brun, court painter to Louis XIV. A third tapestry by de Vos has been sadly mutilated to fit over the chimneypiece by Sir William Chambers: at the opposite end of the room hangs a fairly late portrait of Sir Osbert by the American painter, James Fosburgh; beneath this is a fine red tortoiseshell cabinet from the Antwerp workshop of the Forchardt family, *c.* 1650. On an easel in the south-east corner is a beautiful portrait of Lady Ida at the age of 19 (she was married at 17 and gave birth to Edith at 18), by Sir William Blake Richmond, better known as a Pre-Raphaelite artist than a portraitist. Among many other pieces of furniture and *objets d'art* sprinkled across the room we notice two splendid Venetian busts on pedestals of a black man and his lady. On either side of the fireplace two of the four fine mahogany doors with broken pediments lead into the former Billiard Room. The portrait, also on an easel at the present, is of Lady Sitwell by Molly Bishop (Lady George Scott). The floor was stained in 1988 by Paul and Janet Czainski and is a copy of the inlaid floor in the State Bedroom of the Empress Maria Feodorovna in the Pavlovsk Palace near St. Petersburg.

Chimneypiece in the Drawingroom by Sir Willam Chambers (1726-96).

the BILLIARD ROOM

The Billiard Room, a lobby connecting the Great Drawing Room with the Ballroom, was redesigned in 1914 by Sir Edwin Lutyens with coved ceiling, two windows looking out on the Park to the north, a French window in one corner giving on to the garden and a pair of black columns through which one passes into the Ballroom.

The chimneypiece backs that in the Drawing Room and is probably also by Chambers: over it is another conversation piece by Henry Walton depicting three young surgeons who have just qualified and are enjoying a boating holiday in Norfolk, a charming picture bought by Sir Osbert from the descendant of Mr. Lethbridge, the young man in the centre. Between the two large Venetian vases in jasper is a fine Boule cabinet.

The Three Young Surgeons
by Henry Walton.

24

the BALLROOM

The Ballroom stands at the far, eastern, end of the house. Completed in 1808, it is the last of the great rooms added to the Jacobean core during Regency times: once again, Joseph Badger was the architect; the now familiar patterns on the ceiling of feathers and rose wreaths are embellished here with the emblem of the Prince of Wales to commemorate the opening ball given here in honour of 'Prinny' and his daughter, Princess Charlotte. After the party the Regent made his host a baronet and sent him the bust of the Princess that is still kept here. The room was also contrived to show off the rest of the Brussels tapestries collected by Sitwell Sitwell during the French Revolutionary period: two flank the fireplace, again the work of Chambers, and face the five windows that look south, into the garden. Nowadays, however, the commanding feature that confronts one on entering the Ballroom is the huge canvas that occupies the end wall: *Belisarius in Disgrace*, a masterpiece of Salvator Rosa (1615-1673), probably the finest

25

Belisarius in Disgrace by Salvator Rosa.

picture at Renishaw and once much admired by Thomas Jefferson. This great and sombre painting shows Belisarius blinded and begging for alms but still wearing the trappings of a Byzantine - or, rather, a Roman - general, and is enhanced by a splendid baroque frame attributed to William Kent: the single-headed Prussian eagle records this as a gift from Frederick William I, King of Prussia to 'Turnip' Townshend (1674 - 1738), 2nd Viscount,

famous statesman and later agriculturalist, from whose descendant Sir Osbert made this purchase. We hope visitors will admire the huge Derbyshire Blue-John urn of about 1800 bought by Penelope and Reresby soon after they acquired Renishaw. The room also contains much of the second Sir George's collection of Italian furniture: a pair of enormous Venetian chairs placed on either side of Belisarius and attributed to Andrea Brustolon; a set of 18th century lacquered chairs, also Venetian; two commodes by Maggiolini, one signed, a pair of giant candlesticks said to have been taken from the cathedral of Lucca and an assortment of cabinets - one is, in fact, German, having been made in Augsburg with metal *repoussé* work and which has recently been restored. Before leaving we observe various paintings on the wall with doors back into the Billiard Room: a curious Holy Family with Saints *that is trying to be by* Bassano, a Saint Jerome, complete with the 'Good Book' (his own translation), spectacles, cardinal's hat, 'memento mori' skull and tame lion, by the Flemish artist Marinus van Reymerswaele - both these pictures have been 'long in the house', according to old inventories

- also a fine landscape probably by Marco Ricci. Incidentally, this room was re-painted in 1975 and new curtains and pelmets made in the year 2000. The carpet is a modern French savonnerie. To view the Main Stairs we must traipse back through the Billiard Room and in and out through a corner of the Great Drawing Room.

One of two enormous Venetian chairs attributed to Andrea Brustolon.

the STONE HALL *and* MAIN STAIRS

The Stone Hall is in reality the old staircase well, bereft of flights to the first floor when the second Sir George put in the new Main Stairs round the corner at the end of the 19th century: overhead are flights leading to the 'Duke's Landing' or 'Ghost Passage' that connects the rooms lying over the Great Drawing Room, Billiard Room and Ballroom just visited. The present Main Staircase is an early innovation of the second Sir George - the famous eccentric - and reveals his antiquarian predilections. Many visitors are deceived by this essay in fake Jacobean, so convincing are the newel posts, each carved with an appropriate heraldic beast or other device. However, the pictures hereabouts are more important: for, against the walls of red felt are displayed a series of paintings of horses and hounds, six or seven of them by J. F. Herring (senior), who is said to have started life as a stable lad at Renishaw. The central picture in the group shows the first Sir George with his huntsman, Jack Jones, both in green hunt livery and on horseback with their hounds by the kennels - long since converted into cottages. Also on the stairs are a portrait of Alice, first wife of Sir Sitwell, by Sir William Beechey, *The Post Girl* by Henry Morland and an engaging old view of Derby by a 'primitive' artist of *c.* 1690.

THE PERFORMING ARTS GALLERY

Created to thrill, stimulate, capturing the excitement, a panoply of colour, range and movement, the vibrancy and life of the world of theatre and music.

THE COSTUME GALLERY

The Costume Gallery holds a collection of elegant dresses and uniforms, giving an insight into life at Renishaw Hall over the years.

THE JOHN PIPER EXHIBITION

The John Piper exhibition displays some of Piper's finest works. His pictures combined the mood of the time with architectural delicacy.

THE NATIONAL COLLECTION OF YUCCAS

The recently restored 'Orangery' houses 'The National Collection of Yuccas', a collection of rare plants from the Arizona desert region. The 'Orangery' overlooks the site of the old kitchen gardens, now a nature reserve, and is circled by 'Lady Ida's Walk'.

THE MUSEUM OF SITWELL MEMORABILIA

The Museum of Sitwell Memorabilia gives an insight into the creative and colourful lives of Edith, Osbert and Sacheverell Sitwell. Throughout the 1920s they were at the forefront of the artistic new-wave, introducing to Britain such artists as Picasso and Matisse. Literature and the theatre also drew upon their talents throughout their lives.

the GARDEN AND PARK

Diana by the sculptor Caligari, a Neapolitan, and friend and contemporary of the Venetian artist Tiepolo.

The garden at Renishaw and the great lake below are the creations of Sir George Sitwell and are a fitting memorial to his skill and taste. The yew hedges and pyramids begin on either side of the lawn in front of the house, and are continued on the lower terrace and around the two formal ponds. In the Gothick 'Temple' - a ruined aviary - Sir George placed a Venetian wellhead: elsewhere he installed a pair of marble fountains and various statues - the two best are *Diana* and *Neptune* by Caligari, a Neapolitan, friend and contemporary of Tiepolo.

The 'jockey' on the weathervane over the Stables bears the colours 'green, orange cap' last recorded for Sir Sitwell Sitwell in 1810 and now held by his descendant. The classical Stables with fine Tuscan portico were built by Joseph Badger, as noted, in 1795: he also built the pretty little Dairy or 'Round House' about 1806, the Gothick Temple, part of Coldwell Cottage, and part of Mill Farmhouse, which also sports a *cottage orné* façade by Renishaw Park Golf Clubhouse. John Platt of Rotherham was the architect of Mount Pleasant, once the family house in Sheffield, an attractive red-brick building with stone pilasters; the Gothick Archway, former lodge on the Renishaw approach drive, was designed by Sir Sitwell Sitwell himself, whereas the Golf Clubhouse is an oddity, part mediaeval, part 17th century and part by Lutyens. A novel feature at Renishaw is the vineyard, begun in 1972, planted in the old Top Paddock, where Sir Sitwell Sitwell had his racehorses exercised and, for many years, the most northerly vineyard in western Europe, being on latitude 53 degrees 18 minutes North.

Apart from the garden, kitchen garden and vineyard, 600 acres of woodland are in hand, otherwise the estate consists mainly of tenanted farmland. The old custom of rent dinners is maintained: twice yearly the farmers troop into the Front Hall to be eased of their cash by the agents and be given dinner afterwards by the squire.

And here we must pay tribute to the Hollingworth dynasty, whose wise stewardship did so much to preserve this heritage: William Hollingworth, a quarry owner, acted as part-time sub-agent from 1875. He was succeeded by one of his sons, Maynard, first sub-agent and later agent to three generations between 1899 and 1966, followed by his son, Peter, who began work in the estate office in 1934, and retired fifty years later.

The estates are now managed by the firm of Shuldham Calverley based at their headquarters at Retford.

To the south of the house lies Renishaw's Italianate Gardens, laid out at the turn of the 20th century by Sir George Sitwell, grandfather of the present resident Sir Reresby Sitwell. The sculptured yew pyramids and hedges forming large walls and gateways are delicately softened by rare and unusual plants, giving the garden a true sense of tranquility. Around every corner awaits a surprise, 'The Two Giants', carp-filled ornamental water features, Gothick 'temple' and hidden gardens. Colour co-ordinated flowering borders of *delphiniums*, *phlox*, *tradescantia* and *agapanthus*, to name but a few, form splashes of colour and texture. The whole experience is a real plantsman's treat.

Below the gardens can be found the lakeside woodland walks that take visitors through an avenue of *camellias* and mature woodland, past caves and around the Renishaw lake. A most beautiful place to explore.

"*A garden as beautiful as any in England.*"
Yorkshire Post.